The Abominable Snowcreature

The Abominable Snowcreature

BY STEPHEN RUDLEY

Franklin Watts
New York | London | 1978

Photographs courtesy of:

Royal Geographical Society: pp. 52, 65
The London Times: p. 55
United Nations: pp. 34–35
United Press International, Inc.: p. 26
Wide World Photos: pp. 4–5, 29, 44

Grateful acknowledgment is made to:

Edward W. Cronin, Jr.,
for permission to reprint excerpts from "The Yeti,"
published in the *Atlantic Monthly*,
vol. 236, no. 5. Copyright © 1975.

E. P. Dutton,
for permission to reprint excerpts
from *Bigfoot:*
the Yeti and Sasquatch in Myth and Reality
by John Napier. Copyright © 1972 by John Napier.

Library of Congress Cataloging in Publication Data

Rudley, Stephen.
    The abominable snowcreature.

    Bibliography: p.
    Includes index.
    SUMMARY: Discusses the various sightings of the
abominable snowcreatures or Yetis throughout the
years, their natural environment in the Himalayas,
and their possible evolution.
    1. Yeti—Juvenile literature. [1. Yeti] I. Title.
QL89.2.Y4R83   001.9′44   78–5042
ISBN 0–531–02212–9

To Cynthia and Slugger

Contents

The Abominable Snowcreature

Nepal: November 8, 1951

Late afternoon. The screaming wind dies down, leaving the four figures in a sudden silence broken only by the slow, steady crunching of heavy boots through crusted snow. The bright reds, yellows, and oranges of their expedition gear leap out from the sun-drenched white of the glacier. From a distance they look like four strange insects, out of place here at the top of the world, surrounded by the Himalayas, the highest mountains on the planet—among them Dhaulagiri, Annapurna, Lhotse, and Everest.

The mountains seem unreal, too awesome to be anything but the product of a dream. They are as incomprehensible and as real as the valley that stretches westward toward infinity, its lush green floor falling off thousands of feet below, finally melting into the misty blue light of yet another distant range.

Far up on Menlung La Pass, at an elevation of 19,000 feet

The Himalayas continue to lure mountaineers from around
the world. In 1963, this U.S. expedition crossed Khumbu Glacier
at an altitude of about 18,500 feet (5,612 meters)
on its way to the summit of Mount Everest.

(5,791 meters), the Mount Everest Reconnaissance Party stops and gathers around a set of strange tracks pressed through the deep snow. One of the men points down the side of the glacier, and while the eyes of the others follow, he mumbles something that is lost as the wind picks up again. Changing direction, the party follows the trail of prints down the glacier for almost a mile, where the snow cover thins out to less than one inch. The group stops again. The expedition leader takes off his pack and pulls out a camera. The tracks are photographed. The camera is replaced. The pack is taken up and the party heads off to find a secure spot to make camp for the night.

December 6, 1951. THE LONDON TIMES
A MYSTERY OF EVEREST:
FOOTPRINTS OF THE ABOMINABLE SNOWMAN
by Eric Shipton, Leader of the Reconnaissance

. . . At four o'clock we came upon some strange tracks in the snow. Sen Tenzing immediately pronounced them to be the tracks of "yetis" or "Abominable Snowmen."

. . . The tracks were mostly distorted by melting into oval impressions, slightly longer and a good deal broader than those made by our large mountain boots. But here and there where the snow covering the ice was thin, we came upon a well-preserved impression of the creature's foot. It showed three broad "toes" and a broad "thumb" to the side. What was particularly interesting was that where the tracks crossed a crevasse one could see quite clearly where the creature had jumped and used its toes to secure purchase on the snow on the other side.

I have in the past come across many of these strange tracks, in various parts of the Himalayas and in the Karakoram, but I have never found any so well preserved as these. Sen Tenzing claims that two years ago he, together with a number of other Sherpas, saw a "yeti" at a distance of about 25 yards [23 meters] at Thang Gothi. He describes it as half man, half beast, about 5 feet 6 inches [1.7 meters] tall, covered with reddish-brown hair but with a hairless face. Whatever it was that he saw I am convinced of his sincerity. That night as we were settling down to sleep he remarked: "As no one has ever been here before, the yetis will be very frightened by our arrival." I was relieved by this assurance!

Among Himalayan peoples snowcreatures are ancient history. The Nepalese, Bhutanese, Sikkimese, and Tibetans accept them matter-of-factly. If you were to ask Bhutanese villagers what wild animals you could expect to find in their country they would answer simply: "We have many such animals. We have bears, snow leopards, yetis, monkeys, civets, and many others."

This has not been the case in the West. It took the publicity surrounding Eric Shipton's sharp and perfectly exposed photographs to catapult the Abominable Snowcreature into the limelight of Western press and fancy. (It was not the first time. A wave of snowcreature interest was generated following a reported sighting in the 1920s, but eventually died out.)

In fact, since 1832 many Westerners, mostly Britons journeying through the Himalayas in pursuit of sport and adventure, had reported sighting the creatures or their footprints. Many of them were highly respected mountaineers and competent naturalists; men who were well established in their fields, with excellent reputations. Yet the Abominable Snowcreature was relegated to the file of imaginative tales brought back from the East. Not much attention was paid to them. They were not taken seriously by anyone, especially not by the scientific community.

It was too easy to dismiss these reports as stemming from the effects of the high altitude on the Western mind, or by strange goings on in the atmosphere, or simply fatigue. One photograph changed all that. It could not be dismissed. It demanded an explanation. Eric Shipton, distinguished and experienced mountaineer, obviously wasn't stoned on the altitude. Something or someone was walking the mountains.

7

Are They or Aren't They? The Controversy

Are there really human-like beasts or beast-like humans alive and well in 1977 on the slopes of Everest? The controversy, ignited in full force over two decades ago, rages as fiercely today. Many scientists and laypeople seem to dismiss the Abominable Snowcreature as an impossible fantasy. A few, because of what they have seen, strongly disagree: their personal experiences with the creatures have forced them to believe. Most people fall into a middle category, neither disbelieving nor totally accepting. They need more information before they can make their minds up once and for all. But no matter what the belief, all agree that the existence of snowcreatures is improbable and amazing.

Why have the snowcreatures touched us so deeply? Why has the question of their existence caused such an emotional controversy in our culture? Perhaps it is precisely because they are

8

so improbable and mysterious. The human race has always had a deep-seated need for the unknown, the strange, and the fantastic. Mystery is a very powerful driving force in the human psyche: we crave it. Perhaps unconsciously we feel that too much has been explained away for us today. Science tells us why we are what we are, and why we feel what we feel—tells us until it seems we have been robbed of something important, something private that no one has the right to.

In this light the snowcreatures are renegade escapees keeping the flame of mystery alive. Their existence is a monkey wrench cast into the life-grinding machine, bringing it to a halt. It is as if they were our scream for freedom from bondage to twentieth-century science and logic.

Harriman State Park, New York, is a very tame and popular natural reserve about one and a half hours from New York City. I was alone. The sun dipped behind the clouds, making me ever-so-slightly uneasy. I continued bushwhacking across the gentle mountain slope. Suddenly I heard a rumbling, creaking roar behind me.

I froze. Time stopped. I felt my knees quiver. My ears sharpened. My eyes were hawk's eyes. I felt as though someone had unscrewed the top of my head and poured ice water inside me: the chills started at the back of my neck and went down to my toes. As soon as they subsided I began to look for the . . . the what? . . . the bear? To make that sound it would have to be 16 feet (4.87 meters) tall, with an enormous barrel chest.

I was sure that something was watching me, waiting for me. I strained every muscle in an effort to prevent myself from breaking into a run, felt terror attacking me from behind, was afraid to look back—and unable not to. As I turned a gust of wind pushed against the tall dead tree behind me. It took only a sec-

ond to realize that it was the tree's creaking that had done me in
—this time.

The Abominable Snowcreature. Myth or reality? Monster or
make-believe? It is a mystery we crave and fear at the same
time. The creature emerges from the terror-filled wilderness
and vanishes again, becoming one with our ancient fears of the
unknown.

Where do these feelings come from? Have groundless and
empty fears of the terror "out there" driven people to create
myths, or has something else been at work? There is something
powerful and frightening about the woods and forests, something big that makes us feel small in comparison. It is an environment that tends to bring out those hidden fears that lie
fallow within us most of our waking hours. But what is behind
the fear?

Perhaps these age-old fears have a story to tell us. It may be
that our fears have been well-founded. So-called mythical monsters have sprung from this fear ever since humans first walked
the earth. Perhaps the world-wide occurrence of monster-myth-
terror is a result of the collective unconscious of the human
race recalling the ancient times in our history when mammoth
predatory animals were very real threats. The myths may recall
times when we had to compete with these creatures for food and
shelter, perhaps before humans had learned about the power
contained in fire, club, and stone. In those ancient times an animal roar behind you probably signaled the fact that you were
about to provide a prehistoric carnivore with its dinner.

It is through this hazy world where myth and reality have
overlapped that we must hunt the snowcreatures. It is interesting that the reports of these creatures come only from environments that could actually support such a form of life. Most of
the habitats are in or near mountain forests. This is to be ex-

pected for a real animal fleeing encroaching civilization: it needs a safe place to hide. The isolated mountain wilderness provides it.

Assume for a moment that the Abominable Snowcreature actually exists, and that it was once very common on our planet. As humans gained dominance over the earth, these ancestral creatures would have been driven out from the more hospitable habitats and forced to seek refuge in the most isolated and difficult ones. Life was more demanding here but not impossible. At least they were safe. Over the eons their numbers dwindled, their populations declined, but the species managed to remain intact. It would be in just such environments that the "myths" about them would persist longest—precisely because they are the last places on earth that real "monsters" can or do exist today.

On the other hand, if the snowcreatures are not real, the prevalence of snowcreature mythology in wilderness areas probably results from a meeting of the primary requirement of all mythical monsters: a place to mysteriously vanish into. The mountain forests easily meet this requirement. Our question is, did the wilderness give birth to a world-wide monster myth? Or was it the other way around, with real monsters generating fear of the wilderness and the resultant myths? If we could answer this question we would have a clue to the mystery.

Science and the Snowcreature

Since first graced by the power of thought, people have searched for a system of beliefs with which to order their chaotic world. Magic, mysticism, religion, art, and science have all been usurped in this drive for understanding. In different eras and cultures each of these paths has offered the hope of revealing to human beings both the workings of the universe and their place in it.

At times it has seemed that science could, and inexorably would, break down every conceivable problem into finite bits and pieces and then measure, weigh, and relate each in turn until a solution emerged. The knowledge gained from this analytical attack would then be turned to practical purposes. Advances in modern medicine—organ transplants, heart surgery, vaccines —along with the majesty of moon shots and space probes and the blinding power of atomic energy have acted in concert to instill in us a sense of reverential awe for science.

Today when we ask "Is it true?" or "Is it real?" or "Does it really happen that way?" we look to science to answer. We depend on scientific knowledge to tell us what is and is not, what is possible and impossible. Naturally, in trying to decide on the reality of the Abominable Snowcreature, we would first think of rushing to the scientist for an answer. When this was done over twenty years ago the reply was unanimous: ". . . it cannot exist . . . must have been a bear . . . or a langur [a kind of monkey]."

At present the creatures whose existence we are questioning are not recognized by the scientific community. Snowcreatures are not recorded in any zoological textbook. This omission from the literature carries with it an attendant weight: if it isn't in the textbooks it cannot be real. We must keep this bias in mind. The snowcreature starts out as an underdog. It has been stamped UNSCIENTIFIC and cast aside, dismissed by scientists as a tale believed in by the childish, the primitive, and the ignorant. According to accepted scientific beliefs there is not supposed to be a two-legged human-like beast alive on the planet. If such a creature were to be found we would be forced to rewrite evolutionary theory.

Some of us have begun to look at and question science in a slightly different light. Does science know everything? Can it explain all? Does it make mistakes? Does it change its mind? Should we accept its judgments blindly, or challenge them fiercely? When you begin to explore the history of science and talk to working scientists, a picture of this discipline emerges that is very different from that held by the general public or taught in our schools.

13

Scientists with a sense of perspective are the first to tell you how little is actually known. Despite the dramatic technological advances that have taken place, we still have only a small backbone of pure theoretical knowledge. Technology can make and do things that science cannot understand. Take something as simple as aspirin. We can manufacture as much of this chemical (acetylsalicylic acid) as we please. Doctors know *that* it works but not *how*. Then too, many of our theories are either incomplete or contradictory, and all, as the informed scientist knows, are only temporary. Truth and fact in science change with time. What is considered totally impossible today may become commonplace in ten years' time, or a hundred. What we accept today may be discarded completely tomorrow.

Once the earth was believed to be at rest in the center of the universe. Problems arose that were difficult to explain in this celestial framework. The pursuit of these problems led Copernicus, a Polish astronomer, to propose his controversial theory which declared that the sun, not the earth, was the central body in the cosmos. The years passed, more discrepancies arose, and other scientists proposed that the sun is just one of billions of stars; that neither the earth nor the sun is at rest, but that each is rotating and revolving at fantastic speeds through an incomprehensibly vast universe. Each of these concepts was a rebellion against a basic tenet of established scientific thought.

In the twentieth century, problems concerning the nature of light and other forms of electromagnetic radiation led to a revolution of thought in physics resulting in the creation of quantum theory. Other scientific enigmas spurred Einstein's development of relativity theory which stated that length, time, and mass all change with the motion of a body in terms of a reference point. These theories pushed our concept of the possible beyond anyone's wildest expectations. At the same time they generated new problems and inconsistencies that have shown scientists how little they actually know—how inaccessible and surprising the natural world can be.

Today the Abominable Snowcreature poses yet another problem to scientists. A riddle beckons solution, but the challenge has not been accepted. The scientific community has refused to undertake a serious and determined investigation of the Abominable Snowcreature. We can only guess at what surprises such an investigation would have in store for us, what new ways of seeing the natural world would be opened to us. But science has not responded.

Things of importance, among them the Abominable Snowcreature, are slipping through the net of science. The awareness of this limitation has led people to turn to the wisdom of the East and the seemingly bizarre to complete a picture of life with all its possibilities. Over the last decade there has been a surge of anti-establishment scientific feeling that has taken root in several diverse areas of inquiry, among them UFO phenomena, parapsychology, ESP, organic medicine, acupuncture, Eastern religion, mind-expanding drugs, and the body awareness therapies. All have pointed to an understanding that science alone cannot account for the varieties of experience encountered by human beings.

Perhaps by responding to seemingly unscientific phenomena, science can once again expand its own limits. The Abominable Snowcreature offers just such an opportunity.

Where Can They Hide?

"Snowcreatures simply cannot be real. There is no place left on the planet for them to exist undetected by modern science. Surely, if these creatures were real, scientists would have come across them long ago."

Remarks such as these are frequently heard when the subject of snowcreatures is brought up for discussion. It often seems as though modern communication and transportation technologies have shrunk the world to baseball size. The bulldozer and the chainsaw have cut deeply into the wilderness. It does not seem possible for a large animal to have escaped our attention when so much of the earth's surface has been explored, mapped, and thoroughly combed for all signs of life. Haven't these all been safely stuffed and neatly catalogued in our museums, or locked up in our zoos? The answer is no. Of course, we have discovered much of the wildlife that exists, but not necessarily all.

There is actually still much unexplored land left on the planet —places where no human being has ever been, places capable of supporting fairly hefty forms of life.

Three-quarters of the earth's surface is covered by water. There are thousands of square miles of ocean floor that have never been seen, millions of cubic feet of sea water through which no human has ever passed. No one can vouch for what life forms are or are not alive and thrashing about in the aquatic depths.

Once ashore, there are many places where we can find enormous stretches of equally unknown land. There are the vast forests of northern Canada, and the taiga of Russia; the isolated forests of the Pacific Northwest; the jungles of the Amazon and Congo basins; parts of India, Ceylon, Malaya, New Guinea— and on and on. We are dealing with huge areas of uncharted terrain.

In the United States, in California, Washington, and Oregon, there are over 50,000 square miles (80,500 square kilometers) of such unexplored wilderness. For several hundred miles south of Portland, Oregon, along the coast, one encounters valley after valley and ridge after ridge of deserted conifer forest. No roads, no houses, no people—just the mountains and the trees and the creatures that live among them.

Before the reported sightings of Bigfoot (the American version of the Abominable Snowcreature), there was virtually no reason for anyone to pay attention to this wilderness area. There were no challenging mountains to conquer, not too much to hunt or trap. The only people who came were the loggers and their road-building crews. But the lumbermen had work to do. They were paid to cut timber, not to explore. Besides, they stuck to the access roads. How far into the forest can you see from a road? How easy is it to leave the road and bushwhack for any great distance? If you have ever been in the woods you know the answers to these two questions: not far and not easy. Even well-traveled wilderness areas are known only along the paths, leaving much unseen and unexplored territory. Who therefore can say what creatures are roaming these wilds?

Our planet still has room enough for unknown and mysterious creatures. A brief glance at the annals of science reveals that such unexplored areas have yielded a host of creatures thought to exist only in folklore, to be extinct, or to be nonexistent.

In 1960, a large herd of the wood bison was discovered roaming the Canadian Northwest. They were found not more than 100 miles (161 kilometers) from a reservation thought to contain the last remnants of the enormous oxen. Another, even larger ox, the Kouprey, wasn't discovered by modern science until 1938, in Indochina. Scientists scoffed at the first reports of these creatures, called them unreal, claimed that if they were anything at all, they had to be a cross between two other known species. The scientists were mistaken. The second largest land animal in the world was not discovered until 1910: Cotton's Cerototherium, or white rhino, found in Africa. The Congo Peacock wasn't discovered until 1936. The Komodo Dragon— a large, live lizard fitting mythical dragon-like descriptions— turned up on an island off the Malay Peninsula in 1912.

The kraken wasn't accepted as a real creature until about 1870. Before that time it was believed by scientists to be a mythical sea monster—and a real sea monster by those sailors who had seen them. It was described as looking like an uprooted tree, being round, flat, and full of arms. It was supposed to attack ships and pull them under with these arms. Today we call these arms tentacles, and call this sea monster the giant squid.

For two hundred years, up to the middle of the nineteenth

century, reports of the existence of hairy wild people had been trickling across from Africa. As usual, the European scientific community regarded these as mere figments of childish imaginations. In 1625, the British adventurer Andrew Battell's posthumous description of the beast was published:

> ... The greatest of these two monsters is called Pongo ... This Pongo is in all proportion like a man but he is more like a giant in stature ... for he is very tall and hath a man's face, hollow-eyed, with long haire upon his browes ... His body is full of haire, but not very thicke, and it is of a dunnish color. Hee goeth alwaies upon his legs, and carrieth his hands clasped on the nape of his necke, when he goeth upon the ground. They sleepe in the trees, and build shelters from the raine. They feed upon fruit that they find in the Woods, and upon Nuts, for they eat no kind of flesh. They cannot speake and have no understanding more than a beast ... They goe many together, and kill many Negroes that travel in the Woods. Many times they fall upon the Elephants, and so beat them with their clubbed fists, and pieces of wood, that they will runne roaring away from them. Those Pongoes are never taken alive, because they are so strong, that ten men cannot hold one of them ...

Like earlier reports, Battell's story made little impact on zoology. Over the years other Westerners reported the existence of these pongos, but it wasn't until 1847, two hundred years later, that the gorilla was "discovered" and accepted by scientists.

Perhaps the most jarring of all discoveries was that of the coelacanth. This creature, captured alive in the Indian Ocean in 1938, was not unknown to scientists. On the contrary, it had been frequently encountered and well documented. Scientists knew that it had existed up to 70,000,000 years ago, for it was in the rocks of this later date that the last fossils of this fish had been found.

This 5½-foot (1.67 meters) long fish with the bright yellow eye was supposed to be dead. Instead it hobbled across the ship's deck on its stubby fins, bit the captain when his curiosity over-took him, oozed oil from its heavy scales, and finally, several hours later, did what the scientists thought it had done 70,000,000 years ago—died. It took fourteen years for ich-thyologists to get their hands on another one. Ironically, the na-tive fishermen had been catching and eating these living fossils for as long as they could remember.

This fish could live in both salt and fresh water—even swamps. It is believed to have had a world-wide distribution. It is particularly strange then that not a single fossil was found in the rocks of the last 70,000,000 years. Based on this absence from the fossil record, it was perfectly logical for scientists to assume that these fish were no longer with us: perfectly logical, but incorrect nevertheless. Science described the coelacanth as being extinct. But here it was, so improbable and yet so alive.

It is clear that the natural world can still turn an astonishing trick now and then. Every rock has not been kicked over, and every spider, slug, and bug has not been driven into captivity as a result. The world continues to be amazing for those daring enough to venture into it. It is now time for some global ven-turing.

Snowcreatures Around the World

On a 1921 Everest Reconnaissance, some fifty years before Eric Shipton's expedition in 1972, Sir C. K. Howard-Bury cabled a report concerning the observation of several dark forms moving on a large snow field. After viewing the creatures through binoculars the party climbed to the area to investigate. There they discovered footprints much larger than normal human ones. Bury thought the tracks might have been made by a wolf. The Sherpa guides disagreed: they claimed the tracks were made by the Mehtch-kangmi, or the wild man of the snows. The telegraphed report was botched and came across as Metch-kangmi. This was translated a bit too hastily by a well-known Calcutta reporter as being the Tibetan name for Abominable Snowman. This name was seized by the press and caused quite a stir at the time.

I bring this up now because the name of these creatures was,

21

and is, very misleading. "Abominable Snowman" implies an animal that spends its life tramping across desolate snow fields and glaciers. A moment's reflection points out the fallacy of this belief. The snowman could not possibly live its entire life in the snow because it would not find enough to eat. These creatures are comparatively large and require more than two or three mouthfuls of moss or lichens to survive. A search restricted to the snow fields would probably be unrewarding.

The second problem with the term "Abominable Snowman" is that it implies that there is only one kind of male creature being sought. Since the creature is presumed to be a mammal, there must be females as well as males, and based on various reports there are in fact several different types of Snowcreatures possibly prowling the mountain forests. Ivan Sanderson, writer and field zoologist, catalogues four basic groups: the sub-humans of Central and Eastern Asia (the almas); the proto-pygmy types, from Asia, Africa, and South America; the neo-giants of Asia and the Americas (Bigfoot and Sasquatch); and the sub-hominids of Central Asia (the original Abominable Snowcreatures).

As you can see from this brief description, they come in a variety of sizes from pygmy to giant. They also vary in their degree of beastliness or humanness, the almas and pygmys being closer to humans, the Snowcreatures closer to beasts. There is a whole menagerie of creatures that come to light as soon as one begins to search.

Abominable Snowcreature, yeti, Sasquatch, Bigfoot, dzu-teh, mehteh, alma, kaptar, tehlma, dwendi, agogue—from a dozen different areas scattered widely over the earth come the reports of these strange beings. Are they fairy tales, myths, and fantasies? Or do these reports reveal the world-wide distribution of a long-neglected species?

A summary of reportage includes a multitude of different types of encounters, from the discovery of footprints and sightings to battles and abductions. Some of these reports are too fantastic to be believed. Some obviously have been embellished by fantasy, but perhaps there is even a grain of truth behind these. We are in a difficult position. We haven't seen the creatures, their footprints, or even the terrain through which they have moved. We will read reports by people who claim they have. What shall we make of them?

When I read these accounts, I ask myself over and over again, "Are these real?" I would give anything to have been there to see for myself. Then I would really know what to make of all this. At such times one can understand the scientists' demand for evidence that can be reproduced for the viewing of all interested parties. But, alas, this is not the case with the Snowcreature. We can deal only with rather ephemeral second-hand information. We are left with the tantalizing work of deciding who and what to believe in. Who and what to trust.

The northwestern United States and the Canadian province of British Columbia have long been centers of snowcreature activity. The Sasquatch (Salish Indian for "Wild Man of the Woods") and Oh-mah (Huppa tribe for "Bigfoot") have long been known to native Americans. Such creatures are a commonly accepted part of the mythology and natural history of Western Hemisphere natives. The white people first began to record the presence of these strange creatures in their midst in the early 1800s.

One of the earliest and most tantalizing of these accounts comes from Yale, British Columbia. (The area around Yale has been the sight of many subsequent Sasquatch encounters.) One day a peculiar creature was surprised alongside a train track,

23

followed, and eventually captured. A description of the animal ran in a local paper on July 4, 1884:

> 'Jacko' . . . is something of the gorilla type standing about 4 feet
> 7 inches [1.2 meters] in height and weighing 127 pounds [58 kilo-
> grams]. He has long black hair and resembles a human being with
> one exception, his entire body, excepting his hands and feet are
> covered with glossy hair about one inch long. His forearm is much
> longer then a man's forearm and he possesses extraordinary strength,
> as he will take hold of a stick and break it . . . which no living man
> could break in the same way.

Jacko remained in captivity for a while, but no further news about him was reported. What was he? Perhaps he was buried in the wilderness, or maybe his skeleton is lying undiscovered in a musty attic or basement. The skeptics have claimed that Jacko must have been a chimpanzee escaped from a circus, a "wild child" brought up by Indians, or a simple something-or-other. Those who believe in the existence of the Abominable Snowcreature see him as a young Sasquatch. Skeptics counter with the question, "Why hasn't one ever been captured?" At this point we would have to get our hands on the remains to settle the matter.

Since the 1880s the number of Sasquatch/Bigfoot sightings has passed the two-hundred mark. The creatures have been described repeatedly as big, about 7 to 8 feet (2.1 to 2.4 meters) in height. They are broad across the shoulder and deep in the chest, with human-like legs, hands, and feet. The creatures have monkey or ape-like faces with backwardly sloped foreheads, flattened noses, and cone-shaped heads. They are covered with reddish-brown hair and walk upright, much as humans do.

From time to time the paths of humans and Sasquatches have crossed, creating quite a commotion. Albert Ostman of British Columbia claims that in 1924 he was captured and held captive for several days by a family of Sasquatches.

According to Ostman, he was carried off in his sleeping bag like a sack of potatoes. After a long shoulder-borne journey he was dumped to the ground. Crawling out of the sleeping bag, he found himself in a secluded and enclosed valley surrounded by a family of four Sasquatches, headed by an 8-foot (2.4-meter) tall papa. During the entire stay he was unharmed. The Sasquatches appear to have communicated with one another in jibberish-like speech. They treated Ostman to sweet grass and he returned their generosity by offering them snuff. The latter commodity provided him with his escape. The head of the family ate all of it and became ill. Ostman beat a hasty retreat out of the valley. This story is difficult to believe. It is the kind of report that tends to make people laugh at the whole idea of snowcreatures. But even if there is only the tiniest kernel of truth here it is important to unearth it.

Most Sasquatch encounters are not so dramatic. Many in fact are very tame, like the 1955 sighting by William Roe. While exploring in eastern British Columbia he spotted what he thought was a bear. After observing the creature for a while he realized that what he was looking at was no grizzly. It was about 6 feet (1.8 meters) tall and 3 feet (1 meter) across the chest. The ears were human-like, the eyes small and dark, the neck short and thick. He estimated its weight at 300 pounds (136 kilograms). When the creature finally sensed his presence, it turned and walked away. No big fuss, just one of many quiet sightings of a strange animal.

In 1958, the snowcreature made headlines in the United States. Again, although quite well known and accepted by American Indians, the existence of Bigfoot in California came as a shock to skeptics and believers alike. The incident took place in Bluff Creek Valley.

A road crew was bulldozing a new lumber access road into the wilderness. One morning when the chief catskinner, Jerry

A group of Bigfoot hunters claim to have sighted this ape-like
creature while searching an area northeast of Spokane, Washington.
Is the photograph a hoax, or proof that Bigfoot exists?

Crew, went to start his machine he discovered that someone or something had been there before him. The entire area was covered by footprints. These prints were very much like barefoot human prints, except that they were 17 inches (43 centimeters) long. (Get a piece of paper or two and draw a rectangle 17 inches [43 centimeters] long by 7 inches [17.8 centimeters] wide. Make a rough drawing of a foot in this box and you will have an idea of what surprised Mr. Crew.)

At first, Jerry Crew thought someone had played a joke on him. But when he followed the trail of footprints he saw that it went down inclines too steep for a hoaxer to negotiate. When he told his colleagues about the tracks they first refused to take a look, then did so reluctantly. When they saw the tracks, many of the men admitted that they had either seen or heard of such giant tracks before.

About a month later the tracks turned up again. The men became edgy. Ray Wallace, the owner of the contracting firm, began to get angry. He thought that someone was trying to destroy his work schedule and foul up his construction contract. At this time, one of the crewmen's wives wrote to the local newspaper asking if such wild creatures were known to anyone else. The story finally made the headlines when Jerry Crew showed up in the town of Eureka with plaster casts of footprints left by the latest of the creature's visits. The story ran in the *Humbolt Times,* was picked up by the wire services, and became known internationally.

Once the Bluff Creek story was publicized reports of earlier sightings of footprints and creatures began trickling in. Today this area has become a center of Bigfoot activity. Skeptics explain this by saying that the reason so many people now claim to see the creatures is precisely because of the publicity surrounding them. They claim the media have implanted a monster-like

27

figure into people's minds—now they know exactly what it is they are *supposed* to see out there, and so they see it.

On the other hand, it may simply be that now people are on the lookout for Bigfoot. The publicity in the press has focused attention on the Bluff Creek wilderness. As more people go there, the chances of sighting the creature increase.

People who have claimed to see Bigfoot have been severely ridiculed by their neighbors and looked at suspiciously by their employers. Perhaps the publicity surrounding Bigfoot has given people the courage to tell what they know. Whatever the reason, the number of reported Bigfoot encounters has grown. We now have a large body of circumstantial evidence pointing toward the existence of snowcreatures in the United States.

I suppose it is only fitting that the American snowcreature would become a movie star, featured in the film *Bigfoot*. The film's controversial footage was shot by Roger Patterson in October of 1967. Patterson and a friend came upon the creature while on horseback in this same Bluff Creek area. After being thrown from his horse, Patterson managed to grab his camera and, while on the run, began shooting. The film has subsequently been analyzed by several scientists. According to John Napier it seems to point to a hoax of some kind. There are inconsistencies in the creature's build and manner of walk that led Napier and others to suppose trickery of some kind. But Napier adds that there is nothing in the film that *proves* it is a hoax. "What I meant was that I could not see the zipper, and I still can't. Perhaps it was a man dressed up in a monkey skin; if so it was a brilliantly executed hoax . . . Perhaps it was the first film of a new type of hominid, quite unknown to science. . . ." At the moment we do not know.

Though much less common, reports of Bigfoot-like creatures have also come from South America. From Brazil we hear of

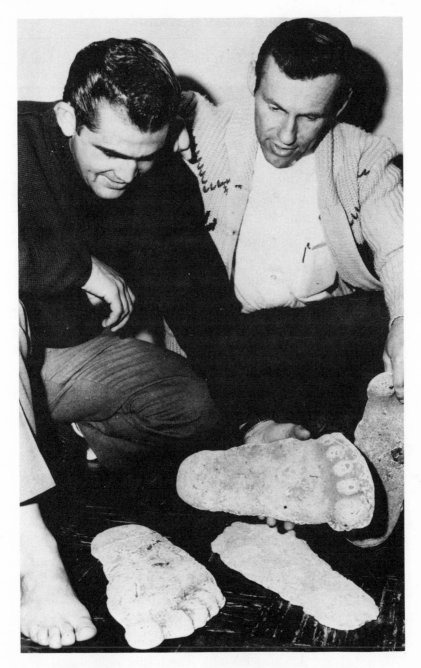

Roger Patterson, right, and Bob Gimlin compare Gimlin's
foot with casts of footprints they claim were made by a
female sasquatch sighted in Humboldt County, California.

the discovery of enormous footprints and the widespread slaughter of cattle whose tongues have been ripped out. The residents there claim that these misdeeds are perpetrated by the giant Mapinguary. Bernard Heuvelmans relates an incident of a man who claims to have been attacked by one. This man, Inocencio, tells of coming across the creature one night in the woods—a thick-set figure "which stood upright like a man." It roared and charged at him. Inocencio fired his rifle, wounding the beast and sending it retreating into the depths of the forest.

From Central America, in British Honduras, come reports of a contrasting type of snowcreature. These are the dwendis— small, semi-human creatures that live in the forests. Ivan Sanderson noted in his travels through the region that dozens of people reported sighting the creatures. These people were "men of substance who had worked for responsible organizations like the Forestry Department, and who had, in several cases, been trained or schooled in Europe or the United States." The dwendis are reputedly 3.5 to 4 feet (1 to 1.2 meters) tall, with long arms and shoulders. They are covered with short, thick hair and have flat, yellowish faces.

We again encounter this pygmy-type snowcreature on the African continent. Here they are called agogues. They are basically human in build, with especially long arms and short legs. Their bodies are said to be covered with reddish-brown hair. Bernard Heuvelmans tells of an incident in which a band of these agogues chased a party of natives from their mountain territory by hurling stones at them.

One final pygmy type must be mentioned: the Orangpendeks of Borneo and Sumatra. (This creature is also called the sedapa, or "little man.") They are believed to stand between 2.5 and 5 feet (.8 and 1.5 meters) tall. Their skin is pinkish-brown and their bodies are covered with dark hair, which is thick at the head and trails behind them like a horse's mane. These sedapas supposedly leave footprints that are small, narrow-heeled, and reversed, with the toes pointing backward and the heels forward. This rather incredible reversed footprint motif is common to snowcreature lore, cropping up in reports about the Sasquatch and agogue, as well as the Himalayan yeti. This sounds like mythology to me, but I will withhold comment on this trait until more information can be gathered.

From this same general geographical area come reports of larger and less tame types. From the Keling Kang Mountains come accounts of a human-sized snowcreature very similar to the descriptions of the Himalayan variety. From Malaya we hear of human-sized and giant types. The latter is the Orang-Dalam, whose footprints have been found in the tropical rain forests around the Endau River. They were measured to be 16 inches (40.6 centimeters) long and 8 inches (20.3 centimeters) wide. The creature is supposed to stand from 6 to 10 feet (1.8 to 3 meters) tall, have a hairy body, and give off a pungent and offensive odor.

Leaving the Himalayas for a later chapter, we turn now to the Asian continent. If you have a world atlas, turn to a map of Asia —one that shows the physical features would be helpful. North of India you will find Tibet. Further north you will see Mongolia, eastward, China, to the west, Turkey and Iran. This is the general area we are talking about. Here from the Caucasus, the Pamirs, the Altais, and Tien Shan Mountains come reports of a whole host of snowcreature types. These include the human-like almas and kaptars, the yeti-like Tok and Golub-Yavan, and the giant Bigfoot variety known as Dzu-teh, or Gin-sung.

Information about the snowcreatures from this corner of the world has not been too easy to get. Research in the U.S.S.R. has not always been in favor with the political leadership, and as a result much of the material was never reported in the newspapers and popular magazines. When the situation changed in the 1960s, Odette Tchernine and Ivan Sanderson were able to contact Professors Porshnev and Rinchen, the two scientists from the Soviet Union who had researched the snowcreatures.

The evidence that these men collected over the years consists of eye-witness sightings and "folk tales," coming from a widespread geographical area and concerning a variety of snowcreature types. They believe that there are probably several "somethings" ranging across the remote Asian mountains.

As an example of what one can find in the Tien Shan Mountains, Odette Tchernine offers the following:

> Stronin's [a Russian geologist] guides were sitting on a rock when he rejoined them. They were very frightened and kept repeating that it had been a Kiik-Kish. [One of these wild creatures had evidently tried to steal Stronin's horses that night.] They flatly refused to accompany Stronin any further.
>
> Stronin later asked the biologists at the Kirghiz Academy of Science . . . about the encounter. They told him there *was* such a creature . . .
>
> . . . In one case two young men . . . saw and photographed tracks of fantastically big bare feet on the shores of a deserted mountain lake . . . A bee keeper . . . was questioned and he stated that according to hunters, there were very big tall men covered with hair that lived in the mountains far up.

It would take several hundred pages to give a full account of the snowcreatures' exploits around the globe. This modest sampling is intended to show that the reports of these creatures are common and quite widespread. Wherever humans have penetrated remote mountain terrain, there have been reports of sightings of snowcreatures. Too many people have seen them, too many strange events have been recorded. We cannot dismiss all of these occurrences with a wave of the hand.

The Snowcreature
in the Land of the Gods:
The Himalayas

It is now time to take a look at the land, inhabitants, and snow-creatures at the top of the world. Take another look at your map of Asia. Sitting on the northeastern border of India is the tiny kingdom of Nepal. To the east lie the even tinier kingdoms of Sikkim and Bhutan. To the north, Tibet. It is in this general area that the Himalayas, the tallest mountains on the planet, are to be found. It is here that the legend of the Abominable Snowman originated. We will focus our attention on Nepal, for it and its mountain people, the Sherpas, are most commonly associated with the snowcreature.

It may surprise you to learn that we know more about the remote Himalayas than we know about some of the mountain ranges in the United States, such as those we have described in Northern California. The Himalayas are well known to the Sherpas, Tibetans, Hindu pilgrims, mountaineers, big game

33

Nepal's rugged terrain deters all but the most adventurous
travelers, and as a result it may provide a safe,
secret habitat for snowcreatures.

hunters (mostly British), and Indian and British civil servants. Many surveys have been made on the geography and topography of the area.

It is amusing to compare the early explorers to modern-day mountaineers who would not think of taking a step without their tents, down sleeping bags, oxygen masks, insulated boots, and sophisticated climbing paraphernalia. John Napier, in his book *Bigfoot*, recounts the experiences of one early Briton who had to make camp one night at 14,000 feet (4,267 meters). He arranged his blankets on a rocky ledge and covered the lot with a waterproof sheet! Later that night he was awakened by a fresh fall of snow. While wondering about the probable depth of snow that would cover him by morning, he took out his trusted umbrella. Apparently his sleep was disturbed by the possibility of losing it to a strong gust of wind.

Nepal rises from the Ganges Plain in India through dense jungles inhabited by leopards, tigers, elephants, and rhinoceri. Journeying northward, one runs into the wild and deserted rainforests that cover the lower Himalayas, which rise a mere 6,000 feet (1,820 meters) from the plains. Beyond lies a mountain range of more imposing dimensions, the Mahabharat, with peaks as high as 10,000 feet (3,048 meters). Crossing the low passes, one descends into the midlands of Nepal, a long, narrow belt of land about 50 miles (80.5 kilometers) wide and 500 miles (805 kilometers) long. It is here that most of the population resides, and the mild climate provides a setting for Nepal's agriculture. Were it not for the mountains, Nepal would have a climate like Egypt's, for it is located at the same altitude. But the mountains are there and one never loses sight of them.

They rise steeply from the central plateau, isolating Nepal from its northern Tibetan neighbors, and halting the flow of flora and fauna from the south. (When you cross into Tibet you find the land populated by a different assortment of plants and animals.) The only way to make contact with the land to the north is through the valleys and gorges of the Himalayan rivers. These gorges are among the deepest in the world. For example, the summits of Annapurna and Dhaulagiri are both over 26,000 feet (7,924 meters) high, and the Kali Gandaki River that cuts between them is only 4,000 feet (1,219 meters) above sea level.

Fossil shells called saligrams are often found in the gorges of the Himalayas. The Nepalese believe them to possess magical powers and believe that gold can be extracted from them. For us, they are proof that the land that makes up the high Himalayas was once undersea. In fact, scientists believe that long ago India was separated from the Asian mainland by the Himalayan Sea. About seventy million years ago the continents started drifting toward one another. Along the line of their collision, the land was squeezed upward to form the giant peaks that are now the Himalayan Mountains.

Here then is the geographical home of the Abominable Snowcreature. There are two questions to be considered. First, is it a suitable home? Does it provide them with shelter? Second, exactly what is it like here and what does it feel like to walk in their habitat? To answer both questions let's see what E. W. Cronin, Jr., has to say. He is a zoologist who spent three years studying animal life in the Arun Valley of Nepal:

The Arun is one of the world's deepest river valleys, an isolated haven for wildlife between the towering massifs of Everest and Kanchenjunga, the first and third highest mountains on earth. Prior to our expedition the valley has remained relatively unexplored because of the rugged topography, inaccessibility, and dense vegetation. Its unique flora and fauna had never been critically studied,

37

and doubtless contained many new species as yet unknown to man. Since numerous reports of the yeti had come from this area, we were open to the possibility that it was inhabited by a population of unknown apes. . . .

These mountains are noted for their ability to isolate populations of animals in steep valleys and protect them from outside competition. Today the Himalayas are truly a biological sanctuary, where creatures long extinct elsewhere continue to live in the inaccessible valleys.

Forests of oak, magnolia, rhododendron, fir, alder, and beech . . . provide an incredible diversity and abundance of plants. Numerous large mammals enjoy the rich conditions there and maintain sizable populations . . . a large primate would do equally well in the Himalayas.

The yeti would have little trouble escaping detection in the steep valleys. The dense vegetation presents a nearly impenetrable wall. During the years I lived in these forests, I repeatedly attempted to leave the trails and travel through the thick, congested undergrowth. My movements were so constricted that I had to force my way through, at times having to rely on a machete to cut a passage. Only a creature born in and adapted to these conditions could travel through the vegetation with ease. It would have been possible for a large mammal to hide within fifty yards of me and remain unnoticed.

The irregular topography would also help conceal a large primate. In the best monster tradition, the yeti could disappear among the numerous gullies, canyons, cliffs, rock shelters, and varied slopes. A two-dimensional map tends to disguise the enormous surface area that exists in the three-dimensional terrain of the highest mountain range in the world. . . .

In addition, these forests are seldom visited by people. The mountaineers hurry to and from their icy peaks and keep on the main trails to facilitate transport of their supplies. The villagers are primarily agriculturists . . . who have little purpose in exploring the forests. There have been surprisingly few naturalists who have spent any length of time in the forests, and even they usually keep to the trails. As in mountain country throughout the world the trails follow the natural signposts of the topography, the ridges and stream beds: the vast area of the slope is virtually isolated.

Now that we have explored the land let us turn to the people. The original inhabitants of this kingdom were negroid. They later mixed with various immigrant tribes, including Mongols, Indo-Chinese, and whites. Today the population of Nepal can be divided into two groups: the Tibeto-Nepalese and the Indo-Nepalese. Within these groups there are several sub-groups, races, and tribes. The peoples of Nepal are a diversified lot. Some, like the Newars, are highly skilled craftspeople who have built many of the pagoda-style temples that dot the land. The Mangars and Gurungs have won fame as warriors: they have a reputation for bravery as a result of their exploits with the British Army in a host of campaigns and wars.

Perhaps the most famous of all Nepalese peoples are the Sherpas. These Tibetan immigrants have won world-wide acclaim for their skills in the high mountains. No expedition to the Himalayas would be possible without them. In addition to their mountaineering skills, the Sherpas are incredibly strong and can carry heavy packloads for long distances. (The main method of transportation in this part of the world is by foot.) Tenzing Norgay, a legend in Nepal and the Western world, was the Sherpa who, with Sir Edmund Hillary, made the first successful ascent of Everest itself.

In the words of Takehide Kazami, a Japanese tourist to Nepal, these people are "as friendly, honest, self-reliant, and hospitable a folk as may be found anywhere in the world." Crime and violence seem to be almost unknown in Nepal. Kazami reports that the poorest of Sherpas may be trusted with enormous sums of money (carried by expeditions to pay porters and guides) and that expeditions making their way through remote areas never have to fear bandits—robberies almost never occur. The Sherpas are also incredibly courteous, sometimes frustratingly so; they so hate to tell you of bad news that at times it is difficult to get any news at all.

The Sherpas are Buddhists (the Nepalese are either Buddhist or Hindu), and the center of their religious life is the monastery. In general, they are deeply religious and are often at prayer, burning butter lamps, spinning prayer wheels and flags. They believe that people are reincarnated, and that the good and bad deeds done in previous lives determine the course of future ones. The Sherpas believe that the people who manage to live enough good lives will finally reach a level of purity that will relieve them of the obligation of having to be born again—unless they want to. They can then volunteer to come back to earth as lamas (spiritual leaders) to help their fellow Buddhists.

The monastery is also the center of learning among these peoples. Ivan Sanderson reports that some of the scholars in these monasteries can speak and write a dozen languages, and have whole libraries of documents and records. "Books published by them five centuries ago on such subjects as history, medicine, and zoology are as precise and as objective as any of our own . . ."

In going to distant lands we often encounter people who have different ways of experiencing and explaining the goings-on in our world. Problems in understanding frequently arise when different peoples try to explain to one another what things are "real." The majority of people alive on the planet have a much wider view on this matter than we sophisticated twentieth-century Westerners. For these peoples, varying gods, plant and animal spirits, rock and water spirits, and human souls are all real in the same way that this book you are holding is real to you. When talking to a Sherpa about the reality of the snowcreatures one has to be clear which (in Western terms) reality we are talking about. The Sherpas have many devils and other beings in their religion, which to them are very real. But these things are not usually considered real by us. We must be careful not to get lost when a Sherpa makes a jump from something that is religiously real to one that is physically real. All I am saying is that we must be cautious. Some scientists have used this problem of realities to claim that all Sherpa reports can be dismissed. I do not share this opinion.

Among the stranger creatures found in the Himalayas are men. What makes them strange to us is the manner in which they pass their days. I am speaking about the Hindu pilgrims, mystics, and Buddhist ascetics who journey and live among the high peaks. There are numerous stories of mountaineers running into scantily clad or naked pilgrims at altitudes of 17,000 feet (5,157 meters) and more. They travel the high caravan routes to their sacred city of Lhasa and the divine mountains in the Kailas range.

In 1930, a British Army colonel came upon one such pilgrim in a blinding snowstorm. The man was clothed in nothing but a loincloth and carried a wooden staff. The colonel called to the man and received the calm reply, "Good morning, Sir, and a happy Christmas." (It was the month of July.) These pilgrims apparently can sleep on the mountains without protection and suffer no ill-effects—this in the same terrain where mountaineers can survive only in expensive expedition-weight down sleeping bags and the finest of nylon tents.

Aside from pilgrims the Himalayas have an indigenous breed of religious monks who are permanent dwellers in the snows. These are the Buddhist ascetics. These men go to the monasteries, where they study a wide variety of subjects that we would regard as supernatural. The psychic abilities of these monks are among the most highly developed of any people on earth. Amazing powers have been attributed to them, including the ability to melt large areas of snow by mere thought alone, being able to transmit their thoughts over great distances, and having the power to transport themselves from one place to another at will. They have gained such mastery over their physical and mental processes that they can exist comfortably in the worst of weather without benefit of clothing or companionship. This lifestyle is beyond most of us. It takes years and years of intense training.

It is in this environment of high mountains and strange men that we must explore the relationship between the Sherpas and the snowcreatures, or yetis, as they call them. For the Sherpas they are as real animals as the yak. Those who have taken the trouble to ask have found out that the Sherpas don't believe that the mountain spirits leave footprints, whereas yetis can and do. For the Sherpas, snowcreatures are physically real beings.

Problems arise when we Westerners attempt to judge the Sherpas' beliefs. On the one hand it is assumed that the Sherpas should know more about the animals in their locality than anyone else since they live there. From this viewpoint we assume that they can tell the difference between a bear and a something-else-that-roughly-looks-like-a-bear—a yeti. But some scientists claim that this isn't so. They point out that the Sherpas, being Buddhists, are not allowed to kill any animals. (They must satisfy their love of yak steaks by importing Tibetan butchers into their country.) As a result they do not hunt leopards, bears, goats, or antelope and are not really that familiar with the habits of these animals in the wilds. Perhaps then they do mistake bears or monkeys for yetis. My belief is that the widespread and consistent stories about the yeti constitute a body of knowledge that separates this creature very clearly from the other Himalayan animals. I believe the Sherpas can tell the difference between a yeti and a bear . . . even though they may be a little too hasty to call all strange tracks yeti tracks and all strange animals the beast itself.

It is difficult to say what the precise meaning of the yeti is for the Sherpas. Investigators have uncovered differing points of view. Some declare it is a commonly accepted belief among the Sherpas that to look at a yeti is to die. Others have reported that the yeti is nothing more than a creature mothers invoke to quiet their noisy children: "Ssh—or the yeti will come take you tonight!" Don Whillans, a mountaineer who had a run-in with a yeti, tells how his Sherpa guides ignored some obviously unusual tracks one day. The experience left him with the impression that the yeti was treated as a sacred animal that one should not pursue, and not be pursued by in turn.

Quite a fuss has been made over so-called yeti scalps. These are found in certain monasteries in Nepal and play a part in several Sherpa dance-dramas. Sir Edmund Hillary persuaded the villagers of Khumjung to give him their yeti scalp so that Western experts could examine it. The initial results of the investigation claimed that the hairs were from an animal called the serow, a Himalayan goat. This led many scientists to dismiss the whole affair. But at least one of the researchers, Dr. William Charles Osman Hill, wasn't so sure that the scalp came from a goat. He saw several features in the strands of hair that were more ape-like in appearance. Even if the scalp turns out to be fabricated from goat hairs it may well have been modeled from a yeti original. For the moment, the meaning of these scalps in the story of the yeti is inconclusive.

The Sherpas and the yeti have met and have established a form of peaceful coexistence. It is clear that this meeting has not been without its embellishments, for the Sherpas love a good

A Lamaist monk displays what he believes to be
the scalp and skeletal hand of a yeti.

story. One hears of Sherpas tracking female yetis whose breasts were so large that they had to be thrown over their shoulders before the beasts could bend over. The Sherpas also know that the best way to escape a yeti is to run downhill as fast as one can—the hapless yeti will be blinded by the long hair falling over its eyes. It was also related, by anthropologist Prince Peter of Greece, how the yeti can be captured by placing a jug of chang (fermented liquor) in its path. The yeti drinks the chang, becomes intoxicated, and is easily captured. Sometimes, but rarely, the yeti has been known to be aggressive. One Sherpa girl told of getting a good look at the beast as it ripped out the throat of her cow and bashed in the heads of her yaks with its enormous fists. Thrown in for good measure are stories of backward pointing footprints supposedly left by yetis. One must remember that exaggerations and embellishments of something do not mean that the something doesn't exist.

They Live: The Sightings

Reports of the existence of the yeti have been drifting out of the Himalayas for centuries, at first from the lips of the Himalayan peoples themselves, and, within the last century or so, from Europeans. The number of natives who have claimed to have seen the creatures or their tracks runs into the hundreds, if not thousands. The existence of three distinct types of snow-creatures emerges from this wealth of data. Two of these are believed to be common to the Himalayas, while a giant variety is spoken about as living in the lands to the north.

The Sherpas' matter-of-fact descriptions of their local snow-creatures include a small creature called the tehlma, found in the lowland mountain forests, and the more robust, human sized mehteh (or yeti) found in the higher altitudes. It is the yeti that has been most commonly encountered and written about. Those who talk about the Abominable Snowcreature are usually re-

46

ferring to yetis. Before we concentrate on the yeti, we should describe the less commonly seen pygmy and giant types.

In 1957, an American expedition was organized to search for the Abominable Snowcreature in Nepal. The goal of tracking down and capturing a yeti was unsuccessful, but Ivan Sanderson reported the following sighting in *Abominable Snowmen: Legend Come to Life:*

> . . . Moving upstream about 300 yards [274 meters] . . . the man came upon a wet footprint on a rock. As he swung his torch low to examine it he saw a snowman on a boulder across the stream, 20 yards [18 meters] away. The Sherpa was terrified, for tales of the yeti in these mountain villages are full of accounts of the creature's strength and habit of killing and mutilating men. He shouted in fright. The beast slowly stood on two feet and lumbered unhurriedly upstream into the darkness.
>
> The following night Gerald's Sherpa guide Da Tempa, a veteran Himalayan tracker . . . went out with the villager. . . . Da Tempa saw movement ahead on the trail. He thought it was probably leaves of a bush rustling, but shone the light at the spot.
>
> There, not more then 10 yards [9 meters] away stood a small ape-like creature, the snowman! The snowman advanced deliberately towards the light, and Da Tempa turned and ran. Next morning Gerald said he found four very clear footprints in the gravel trail, which he photographed. From questioning Da Tempa and the villager these facts emerged about our elusive quarry:
>
> He is about 4 feet 6 inches [1.37 meters] high, with hunched shoulders and a very pointed head which slopes backwards from his forehead. He is covered with thick reddish-grey hair. His footprints are about 4 inches long.

Elaborate plans were devised to capture the creature. Bait was set out in an attempt to lure it to the hunting blinds where the men were hiding. Giant 1 foot-long (30 centimeter) frogs were tied to nylon fishing line and set free in the stream. However, the monsoon season was upon them and the torrential rains turned their nightly vigils into a nightmare. At the same time the rains made tracking the creature impossible. The snowcreature was not captured.

The giant variety of snowcreature is reported to live in the lands to the north and east. This species is called the Tok, kung-la, and Gin-sung. In the Himalayas it goes by the name of Dzu-teh, which can be roughly translated as "the hulking thing." The Dzu-tehs are most similar to the American Bigfoot or Sasquatch, being much taller and heavier than the common yetis. They are reported to be covered with black to dark gray shaggy hair, have flat heads, long powerful arms, huge hands, and human-like feet. The Tibetans tell us that these giants often raid yak herds, and can survive in the most frightful of climates. They are supposed to have the ingenuity of humans coupled with inhuman strength. It is likely that these rugged giants are cousins of the creatures that made their way across Asia and the Bering Strait into Alaska and points south.

We turn now to the yeti. If we were to take all the reports of yeti sightings and reduce them to a single police blotter-style description, we would wind up with a remarkably vivid and consistent "wanted" poster of the yeti. Many scientists have commented on the consistency of these reports, claiming that they point to the existence of a real creature. If the yeti were an imaginary monster then we would expect to find a wider variety of descriptions—unusual growths of hair, fangs, coloration, and other more outlandish features. Instead, the majority of what we consider to be reliable reports depicts a more modest creature that is possible within the present realm of zoology.

The yeti is roughly human sized in height, ranging from 5.5 to 6.5 feet (1.7 to 2 meters) tall, but more robust in build. The body is stocky and ape-like in general shape and is covered by short, coarse hair, reddish-brown to black in color. The face

48

is hairless and somewhat on the flat side. The jaw is very prominent and the mouth quite wide. It has large teeth, but no fangs. The neck is very powerful and is topped by a conical head which comes to a pointed crown. The shoulders are heavy and hunched, the arms quite long, extending to the knees. The feet are short and broad.

The first time the yeti made it into print in the Western world occurred in 1832. B. H. Hodgson, a Briton stationed at the court of Nepal, related how his native hunters were frightened by a rakshas, or demon. The creature walked erect, was covered with dark hair, and had no tail. Hodgson thought little of these hunters who did not stand their ground and shoot the beast in courageous fashion.

Footprints were first reported in the European press in 1887. That year, in the Kingdom of Sikkim, a Major L. A. Waddell of the British Army came across footprints in the snow at about 17,000 feet (5,157 meters). He was assured by his Sherpa guides that the tracks were made by the notorious yeti. Waddell thought the Sherpas were mistaken. He tells of their universal belief in the yeti but relates how he could not bring himself to believe in the creature. He thought a bear had made the mysterious tracks.

Although such reports continued to trickle in, it was not until the mountaineers invaded the Himalayas that the yetis finally received world-wide attention. The first Everest Reconnaissance Expedition of 1921, led by Lieutenant Colonel C. K. Howard-Bury, reported humanoid footprints on a mountain pass at an elevation of 20,000 feet (6,067 meters). The following is his account:

> Even at these heights . . . we came across tracks in the snow.
> We were able to pick out tracks of hares and foxes, but one that first
> looked like a human foot puzzled us considerably. Our coolies at

once jumped to the conclusion that this must be the "Wild Man of the Snows" . . . On my return to civilized countries I read with interest the delightful accounts of the ways and customs of this wild man whom we were supposed to have met. These tracks, which caused so much comment, were probably caused by a large 'loping' grey wolf, which in the soft snow formed double tracks like those of a bare-footed man . . .

Like Waddell before him, Howard-Bury was unable to accept the existence of the Sherpas' yeti. For him the whole affair was blown out of all proportion—a native fairy tale gone wild.

In 1925 the sighting of a "something" caused quite a commotion, perhaps because the man who filed the report was A. N. Tombazi, a well-known photographer and a Fellow of the Royal Geographical Society. The following incident took place at an altitude of 15,000 feet (4,550 meters):

The intense glare and brightness of the snow prevented me from seeing anything for the first few seconds; but I soon spotted the 'object' referred to about two to three hundred yards [183 to 274 meters] away down the valley . . . Unquestionably the figure in outline was exactly like a human being, walking upright and stooping occasionally to uproot or pull at some rhododendron bushes. It showed up dark against the snow and, as far as I could make out, wore no clothes. Within the next minute or so it moved into some thick scrub and was lost to view.

Such a fleeting glimpse, unfortunately, did not allow me to set the tele-photo camera, or even to fix the object carefully with the binoculars; but . . . I purposely made a detour so as to pass the place where the 'man' or 'beast' had been seen. I examined the footprints which were clearly visible on the surface of the snow. They were similar in shape to those of a man but only 6 to 7 inches long by 4 inches [15 to 18 centimeters by 10 centimeters] wide at the broadest part of the foot. The marks of five distinct toes and of the instep were perfectly clear, but the trace of the heel was indistinct, and the little that could be seen of it appeared to narrow down to a point . . . The prints were undoubtedly those of a bi-ped, the order of the spoor having no characteristics whatever of any imaginable quadruped . . .

The description of the footprints led John Napier to assume that the creature involved in this sighting was a bear. Bears leave narrow-heeled footprints while those of humans are characteristically broad-heeled. However, Napier recognized a contradictory element. The creature appeared to have walked on two feet. A bear can stand on its hind legs and be quite comfortable. In this pose it might well be taken for a human. But once on the move there is no problem distinguishing bear from human. Bears do not have an anatomy consistent with two-legged walking. According to Napier, "it is almost inconceivable to imagine anyone, however scientifically naive, mistaking a bear's walk for a walking man." A bear moving on its hind legs is simply too clumsy and grotesque to be interpreted as anything but a bear. Napier assumed that Tombazi must have been mistaken in his memory of the creature walking upright. But what if Tombazi's memory is correct? We might then have to conclude that he saw a creature that science is ignorant of.

Like the American Bigfoot kidnapping of Albert Ostman, an equally fantastic event is supposed to have occurred in the Himalayas. A Captain d'Auvergne had an accident on one of his solitary jaunts through the mountains. Injured and in danger of death by exposure, he was rescued by a giant yeti, carried to the creature's cave, cared for until he was fully recovered, then sent home unharmed. D'Auvergne wrote an article describing the creatures as prehistoric leftovers of human stock that found refuge in the high mountains, where, over the centuries, their bodies adapted to the rugged terrain and climate.

The mountaineering expeditions of the 1950s brought another slew of track-sightings. The men involved in these incidents were all well known and highly respected in climbing circles: Eric Shipton, John Hunt, and H. W. Tillman. All of these en-

In 1951, Eric Shipton provided the first clear, unretouched
photograph of what are purported to be the tracks of a yeti.

counters took place at altitudes of about 18,000 feet (5,460 meters). Some were probably made by known animals, others are more questionable. Unfortunately we do not have a photographic record of these tracks and have little to go on in the way of analyzable material. On two separate occasions Hunt and Tillman came across sets of blurred tracks that appeared to have been made by a two-legged creature, possibly a human. On both occasions there was a second climbing party in the same vicinity. Both times it was assumed that the tracks were made by a member of the other party. When inquiries were made as to which intrepid climber was daring enough to cross the Zemu Pass alone the reply was the same—no one.

The importance of the 1951 Shipton encounter (he had seen similar tracks on previous climbs) with strange tracks in the snow, was the fact that a clear photographic record was taken. The pictures provided scientists with a rare piece of evidence to examine. For scientists it is very important to obtain hard evidence, something tangible that can be investigated and experimented with. The previous snowcreature reportage consisted solely of verbal evidence. We were told that "something" was seen, or told that a strange track was discovered. We had to decide whether or not to trust the individual's honesty, memory, and intent.

Shipton's photograph was different. A photograph can be analyzed in and of itself, though this analysis may prove inconclusive owing to blurriness of the image, lack of proper exposure, or too small a scale. Over the years climbers have photographed supposed yeti tracks, and, after developing the photos, have wound up with blurry, underexposed, and scientifically useless prints. Then too, a photograph may be faked or touched up. But at least we can try to determine this from the film itself, as in the case of the Patterson film of the American Bigfoot, whose authenticity is currently debated. In these cases there is at least something on which to base an objective analysis. The Shipton photograph may be sent out to several laboratories for examination. Different investigators may come up with totally variant conclusions, but each can point to the picture and show why he or she has interpreted the evidence in a particular way. The rest of us can look at the picture and judge for ourselves the sense or nonsense that is being made.

The publicity centered around the Shipton photograph demanded an explanation from scientific circles. The British Museum in London prepared an exhibit which explained the footprints as being those of a langur, a kind of monkey. But as John Napier points out, "In view of what is known of the altitudinal range of the Himalayan Langur, and the impossibility of equating the enormous Shipton footprint (13 in. by 8 in.) (33 cm by 20 cm) with the hands and feet of a monkey whose maximum foot dimensions are 8 in. by 2 in. (20 cm by 5 cm), almost any explanation would have been better than this." The point is, the museum put itself on the line and other people could refer to the photos and tell these experts that their explanation was absurd.

Since the British Museum exhibit, a host of explanations have been offered to account for the existence of these tracks. Among the animal kingdom, bears, monkeys, foxes, and even birds have been suggested, as have all manner of combinations of animals walking the same trail. The possibility of giant tracks being formed by the effects of sun and wind on normal-sized tracks has been explored. Finally, the possibility of the whole affair being an intricate hoax has been considered. A brief look at John Napier's analysis of these ideas as they relate to the Shipton tracks will give you a feel for how difficult the exploration of the unknown can be.

**The giant footprint photographed by Eric Shipton
bears little or no resemblance to the track of any known
creature in that area of the Himalayas.**

As a result of experiments performed in the snow with a track-making device, Napier states that although melting snow can alter the size and shape of a fresh track, there is usually no difficulty in recognizing that melting has occurred. The melting of snow leaves the track with a blurry, woolly appearance. Details in the floor of the track are lost. However, in cases where footprints have overlapped, melting does sometimes destroy the evidence that two prints were involved. It would seem then that *if* the yeti does not exist, these mysterious footprints probably result from double tracking by a known animal or human.

In pursuit of an answer, Napier discovered that the photo published in the press did not include all of the picture as originally photographed by Shipton. He obtained the original negative and made a new photograph. Studying the complete photograph led him to believe that melting had occurred in the area of the heel. This indicated that the track when first formed was narrower in the heel. Since a narrow heel is the opposite of what one would expect from a human-like creature, Napier concluded that the track was not made by a human or "any ape-like creature known to science." In his opinion just about any animal *might* have been responsible for the original print— "a bear, a langur, a fox, a snow leopard. . . ." Napier's final opinion on the matter was that "To some enthusiasts, quite understandably, Shipton's footprint is proof of the existence of the yeti, but to me it is proof of absolutely nothing. I am not prepared to accept it on face value. I do not believe that, as it stands, it is the print of an unknown ape-like creature. I accept that melting and sublimation can convert a fox's pugmark into a vaguely human-like or ape-like footprint, but I am not convinced that this is the whole story. If I had to make a guess— and this is all that it is—I would say that the footprint is composite, made by a naked human foot treading in the track of a foot wearing a leather moccasin . . ."

But before dismissing the yeti as a hoax, we have one more report to consider. It demonstrates how difficult it is to know what is what in the world of the snowcreature.

One day in 1972, on the Himalayan research expedition mentioned earlier, E. W. Cronin, Jr., made a side journey to a remote high-altitude pass. The following morning Cronin was awakened by the excited cries of his companion, Dr. Howard Emery. During the night, or early morning, a creature had walked between their tents, leaving a fresh set of footprints. The Sherpas immediately took them to be those of the yeti.

A complete photographic record was made. The crystalline snow was ideal for displaying the prints. These photographs were taken before the sun had risen. The dimensions of the prints were 9 inches (22.8 centimeters) long by 4.75 inches (12 centimeters) wide, and ". . . These features were present in all the prints made on firm snow, and we were impressed with their close resemblance to Shipton's prints."

(Although not as imposing in length as those of Bigfoot, the tracks of the yeti make up for it in raw power. Compared to both human prints and those of Bigfoot they are much more rough-hewn, much less refined and delicate—more bestial. They have an enormous big toe, an even longer but thinner second toe, and both are separated from the three little toes. They also lack the arch common to the human foot.)

The two scientists followed the trail of prints away from the camp, down a snow-covered slope. After a short distance they had to turn back because "The heavy snow made walking impossible. . . . I was forced to cling to the slope with my hands . . . searching for the prints was arduous and extremely dangerous. We realized that whatever creature had made them was far stronger than any of us."

Zoologist Cronin refers to the similarity between his and Shipton's prints again and again. These similarly constructed footprints occurred twenty years and many miles apart. The earlier set was explained away by Napier as a combination track of foot and moccasin, made to look like one large track because of the effects of sun and wind. But the new set could not have been produced in this way.

Cronin's tracks were discovered and photographed before sunrise. No melting could have occurred. The scientists compared their own day-old tracks to fresh ones and could not see any difference. This allowed them to discount the wind as a footprint retouching agent. (Their own day-old tracks should have been altered in some way if the wind was at work.)

It would seem that the tracks Cronin saw were the same as made by the creature. We have now come full circle, for we must once again explain what single beast could have made these tracks.

Cronin's expedition took special pains to examine all large mammal tracks they encountered. They took photographs of tracks made under differing conditions of snow, terrain, and animal activity. They compared the mystery footprints with all known tracks and came up with the following conclusion:

> As professional biologists with extensive experience in the Himalayas, we feel we can eliminate any possibility that the prints were made by any known, normal animal. . . . I believe that there is a creature alive today in the Himalayas which is creating a valid zoological mystery. It is possibly a known species in a deformed or abnormal condition, although the evidence points to a new form of bipedal primate. Or perhaps an old form—a form that man once knew and competed with, and then forced to seek refuge in the seclusion of the Himalayas.

How They Live:
The Life of the Snowcreature

The controversy continues. One moment the evidence sustains our beliefs, the next it renders them improbable. Since there is no definite proof of this enigmatic creature's reality, perhaps we can try another line of approach. Suppose you have come to believe, as I do, that snowcreatures are real. Could such beasts survive in the environment we imagine them to live in?

Before we account for how they live, we must remind ourselves of where they live. Both the name Abominable Snowcreature and the fact that most of the tracks have been found in the snows of the high Himalayan passes, have generated the impression that they are denizens of the mountain snow fields. If one tries to explain the yeti in terms of this snow-bound environment the conclusion must be that the yeti cannot be real.

Many people have made this mistake. The problem is that no creature could possibly eke out a living from a perennially snow-covered habitat—there would not be enough food. Animals such as the musk ox and reindeer do survive on the snow-bound Arctic lowlands because the snow melts for several summer months, exposing a rich layer of underlying vegetation. In winter these animals can dig through the snow and find nourishment. Not so in the high mountain snow fields of the Himalayas, where the snow cover remains year round.

To survive, the yetis would have to live at more modest altitudes below the tree line. Why then have we discovered so many tracks on the snow fields? Several explanations have been offered. One that has been around for a while is that the yetis, like human pilgrims and mountaineers, are simply on their way someplace else, perhaps to feed in another mountain valley. The evidence of the tracks seems to bear this out. Many of these trails lead from one forested valley to another; they do not appear to continue up toward the higher fields of perennial snows. It is not surprising then that humans have encountered the tracks on the same passes they travel, for most Himalayan creatures must follow the same few routes.

Another explanation held by the Sherpas is that the yetis like the salt found in a kind of moss that grows on the rocks in the snow fields. Ivan Sanderson has pointed out that it may also be the vitamin E content of certain lichens that lures the yetis to the high passes. Sanderson explains that it is vitamin E that drives the lemming to swarm and birds to fly many thousands of miles to the edge of the melting polar snows to breed. The rich vitamin supply contained in the spring vegetation and insect populations provides the young birds with all their nutritional requirements in a concentrated area.

In the Himalayas the snow fields start at about 14,000 feet (4,247 meters). Moving down the side of a typical Himalayan peak one would encounter in succession moorland, rhododendron forest, bamboo forest, dense mountain forest, and then, on the valley floors, tropical mountain vegetation. Each of these kinds of forest could be a possible home for the yeti. Each houses its own combination of plants and animals that could provide food for a large yeti-like primate. In our attempt to explain the snowcreatures, we must first account for how and what they could eat. For the yetis to survive they must be able to find enough food to sustain their rather hefty bulk. What are their chances in the Himalayan valleys? Once we allow their homes at the lower altitudes their chances are excellent.

The question is, just what kind of eaters are yetis supposed to be? There are several alternatives. First, it is possible for them to exist on a basically vegetarian diet, like that of the gorilla. The Himalayan valleys, up to about 6,000 feet (1,820 meters), have much the same kind of year-round food-providing forests as those that the gorilla frequents in Africa. Several scientists believe that the gorilla was originally found in higher mountain forests and only migrated southward when the earth went through its severe climatological changes. Collin Groves even suggests that the gorilla's thick chest and compact build is an adaption to living in cold weather and high altitudes. It is also interesting to note that the African gorilla has been known to ascend to altitudes of 13,000 feet (3,934 meters) in passing from one forest to another. Primates do travel about.

On the other hand, it is possible that the yetis exist as graminivores, animals that subsist on a variety of small, high-energy foodstuffs, such as seeds, roots, and tubers. This dietary style is found in the present day gelada baboon and appears to have been the feeding pattern of Gigantopithecus, a giant fossil ape that may be related to the yeti. (We will investigate this creature in the next chapter.)

The most probable feeding technique for the yetis, which

61

would provide them with the most latitude for survival, is that of the omnivore. An omnivore eats a little of everything: any animals it can catch, any plants it can dig up, fruits, vegetables —anything. Humans are typical omnivores, and so are bears. Each species is adapted in its own way to this style of feeding. Bears have teeth that are suited to eating flesh, as well as sharp claws and powerful limbs for procuring the flesh in the first place, or gathering berries. Humans do not have specialized teeth, but make up for it with their technical abilities to kill and prepare their meals of either animal or plant.

Details of the yetis' feeding habits are unknown. Except for their reputed strength it is unclear how they are specifically adapted for the omnivorous life. There have been reports of yetis attacking yaks and crushing their skulls with their fists. This same brute force is supposed to be used to advantage in their hunting for the pika, or Himalayan hare. The yetis search for these small mammals among the loose rocks on mountain slopes. They crush the hare, rip off its skin, rip out the entrails, and eat the flesh raw. The same terrain produces roots, seeds, fruits, berries, and a host of other plant foodstuffs. It is clear that the Himalayan forests provide an abundance of plant and animal food possibilities—more than enough to support an omnivore of the yeti's size.

The scatological evidence also points toward an omnivorous diet. Scatology is the science that studies animals' droppings, or excrement. Quite a lot of information can be learned from this science. The most obvious is that we can easily find out just what a particular animal has been feeding on. Over the years fecal matter reported to have been left by the yetis has been collected and examined in modern laboratories. Among the typical contents are pika whiskers and bones, bird feathers, grass and other plant matter, as well as insect parts— omnivorous remains.

Another possible explanation linking the feeding habits of the yetis and their tracks in the snow fields is the use of frozen foods. Sometimes animals are found to be a jump ahead of humans in coming to terms with their environment. Naturalist Frank Beebe and anthropologist Don Abbott proposed a feeding pattern for Bigfoot that may apply to the yeti as well. It is based on the strange habits of wolverines. These large weasel-like creatures live in much the same habitat as the American Bigfoot. They have an ingenious method of dietary survival. These animals save certain of their kills, carry them up above the snow-line, and bury them there beneath the snow. When food is hard to find the wolverine returns to its deep-freeze, digs up a meal, carries it down the mountain, lets it thaw, then eats it. If the wolverine can do it, why can't the yeti?

Two other survival techniques have been mentioned in accounting for the yeti's adaption to the problem of food supply: migration and hibernation. Animals that live in habitats that become inhospitable for a part of the year often get around the problem by leaving it. They migrate to another area. Field studies have revealed that some North American black bears leave their inland forests during the winter months and travel to the seashore. Here they get by on a diet of fish and other sea food. Such a feeding pattern was proposed as an explanation to account for Bigfoot's survival. (These larger cousins to the yetis have a more intense nutritional problem. The forests they live in are not as richly populated by plant and animal food sources.) For the yeti, like the Asiatic black bear, migration would probably only mean moving down to the lower slopes and valleys. Here, especially on the valley floors, a rich supply of vegetation can be had year-round.

The second possibility is hibernation. When the cold weather and snow set in, some animals simply "go to sleep." The marmot is an animal that hibernates. When the temperature drops, this animal rolls up into a heat-conserving ball and dozes off. All its vital processes slow down to the absolute minimum needed to keep it alive. Its internal temperature drops, and its heartbeat slows down. The marmot's body chemistry goes into a slow-motion pattern that requires only a fraction of the energy needed to keep it going in its active state. In this way the animal can draw out the food supplies stored in its body and keep itself alive for long periods of time without eating.

Is it possible that the yetis get through the winter months by hibernating? The chances are that they don't. We assume the yetis to be primates (the same group as humans, apes, and monkeys). These animals neither hibernate nor den up as bears do, even in the worst of weather. They usually stand their ground and battle with the elements and with dwindling food supplies.

Since so much stress has been laid on the yetis' footprints, we ought to say something about how the creatures actually make them. What is their style of walking? Reports concerning the yetis, especially those given by the Sherpas, are divided between quadrupedal (four-footed) and bipedal (two-footed) walking. Bipedalism is believed by many to be restricted to humans. If the yetis walk on two feet, they are therefore assumed to be closely related to human beings. Because of this, the question of their locomotion has assumed controversial proportions. It is my belief that the yetis are bipeds. Undoubtedly several reported yeti sightings are really attributable to other animals, notably bears, and these may be the source of the four-footed notion.

Cronin's analysis of the tracks he encountered led him to believe they were made by a bipedal animal. There was no evidence of overlapping in the long trail of prints he examined.

These tracks are almost certainly those of a bipedal creature.
The question that continues to challenge investigators is whether
they were made by some familiar animal or by the legendary yeti.

He also states that two-footed walking is *not* limited to humans. He claims that gibbons and orangutans, two primates that spend most of their time in the trees, consistently walk in the bipedal manner when on the ground. Gorillas adopt the two-footed pattern for short distances when moving over stretches of wet vegetation. Chimpanzees in captivity have taken to bipedal walking when on snow-covered ground. (Presumably this is to prevent their hands from getting cold.) Cronin concludes that it is reasonable to assume that primates living in the high Himalayas would transport themselves on only two feet.

The question of walking style is vital to the yetis' acceptance by the scientific community. If the yetis are bipeds, and if the tracks we call yeti tracks are made by two-footed creatures, then we can rule out the possibility of the yetis really being misperceived bears. The bear has been offered up as the most likely animal behind the yeti myth—by those who believe them to be mythical. Bears live in the same environment, have similar feeding patterns, and are the correct size and general shape for a yeti look-alike. The problem with bears is that they are confirmed quadrupeds. Although they can easily support themselves on two limbs, they walk on four. Their bodies were simply not designed to carry their bulk in an upright fashion. If the sightings of creatures walking on two feet are accurate, those creatures are not bears.

Related to the problems of feeding, locomotion, and general elusiveness is the question of the activity rhythm of the yetis. Animals have varying patterns of rest and activity depending upon their particular environments and lifestyles. Some animals are active during the day and sleep at night. For others the pattern is reversed. Nocturnal animals rest when the sun is out and begin to stir at sunset. A growing number of investigators are now of the belief that the yeti is of the nocturnal disposition. This is somewhat surprising since save one or two exceptions all monkeys, apes, and humans are daytime creatures. It is assumed that early forms of apes and humans were also lovers of daylight. Why then have the yetis taken to their nocturnal ways?

It is quite probable that the yetis have been driven to this lifestyle as an adaption to living in close contact with humans. Many other animals have changed their activity patterns in an attempt to survive civilization's encroachment. The tiger is one such animal. It is thought that tigers were originally diurnal (daytimers) and took to the night to save their skins. At one time in the not-too-distant past the tiger population of India was 40,000. Today it numbers roughly 2,000. Hunting and the cutting down of forests have endangered the very existence of these noble beasts. However, on game preserves the tiger is now protected from both chain saw and gun. Some evidence suggests that these felines are reverting to a pattern of daytime activity.

The yetis' adoption of the nocturnal pattern is probably another reason why they are seen so rarely. While humans are making their way through the forests and over the passes the yetis are safely hidden and resting.

Before examining the problem of where yetis as a group come from, we ought to stop for a moment to consider where a single yeti comes from. The answer to this question is simple and obvious once you think about it. The yeti, like every other animal on the planet, must reproduce itself. We assume that it does so in a way similar to other mammals. Therefore, each yeti must have a male and female parent.

If one yeti exists there must be *populations* of these creatures alive today. As mind-boggling as it is to contemplate the existence of several different types of snowcreature, it is even more astounding to realize that for each different type there must be a corresponding population. No one has any idea of what the numbers involved are; anywhere from hundreds to thousands may exist in the regions of the Himalayas we have been discussing.

A population of yetis means that there is an assortment of males and females in varying states of maturity roaming the Himalayas. Those who doubt the yetis' existence point to the fact that family groups have never been seen. (The American Bigfoot has been sighted in groups, according to some reports.) As things now stand all we can say is that the yeti appears to be a solitary creature. We must assume that the young exist and are kept secluded until maturity, or have been seen and mistaken for other animals. Perhaps the two species of snowcreature that the Sherpas speak about are really one. It may be that the smaller tehlmas and the larger yetis are really the two sexes of the same species. Differences in size between males and females of the same type of animal are a common occurrence in nature.

There is not much that can be said about the yetis' daily life. Our knowledge about animals in the wilds comes from patient and prolonged field studies and laboratory analysis. It takes years of hard work to begin to amass enough information to build a life history of any animal, let alone one whose very existence is in question. All we can do is wait . . . and hope.

Where Did They Come From? The Evolution of the Snowcreature

Like other plants or animals, yetis must have an evolutionary history. Those of us who accept yetis as present-day creatures must be able to account for their origins. If we can show where and how yetis fit into the development of humans and apes, it becomes easier to accept them.

At a point in time many millions of years ago, the evolutionary line that was to lead to humans separated from that of the apes. The pongidae (apes) went one way and the hominidae (humans) went another.

Many theories have tried to explain the hows and whys of this parting of the ways. Whatever the reasons, when our ancestors dropped from the trees and took to the savannas, they did so in two-footed fashion. In fact, bipedalism as the basic means of transportation is one of the most important features separating human beings from the rest of the animal world. Chimps, gibbons, and gorillas can walk on two feet when required, and do so when it helps to solve a temporary problem. But the fact remains that of all the primates, the hominidae seem most completely adapted to two-footedness. In turn, two-footed walking is *essential* for their way of life.

Footprints of apes and monkeys show signs of a life lived in the trees. Their feet are all equipped with an opposable big toe, enabling them to curl their toes around tree branches. In contrast, the feet of humans clearly have been long adapted to a life firmly planted on the ground—no opposable big toe, no need to clutch branches any more. The feet of humans have developed into their only weight-supporting appendages. In so doing they have freed the hands for other uses—uses that have been crucial to the emergence of the human being we see today.

Once the transition from tree to savanna was made, a steady pressure for two-footedness developed. There are two reasons for this. First, life on the ground proved much more treacherous than arboreal living. From the branches it was easy to spot danger. Among the shrubs and grasses self-protection was a more demanding affair. It was soon discovered that the eyes would provide the best advance warning of danger the higher they were lifted. The head and eyes of the erect human were therefore placed in the best protective position. From this point on, any anatomical development that helped to support an erect body and upright gait were clearly advantageous.

The second pressure for two-footedness was related to the hands and what could be done with them. Once on the ground there were berries to be picked, seeds to be gathered, roots to be dug for, and insects to be plucked from the bark. The arms, hands, and wrists of these early primates had already been well-developed by a life among the branches. They were quite powerful and dexterous, well adapted to supporting the body's weight as it moved through the trees. Further, the arms were perfectly coordinated with the eyes. Three-dimensional vision was crucial for judging distances from branch to branch. Coordinating eye and hand movements was a highly sophisticated function of the brain, capable of expanded activities. This expansion was speeded up when these early primates landed on the ground.

Further along the evolutionary line, another advance occurred. What may have happened was that one day one of these creatures spied a tasty insect and reached for it with his or her hand—the same one that happened to be holding a twig. Suddenly, there was the beetle impaled on the point of the "spear." The creature caught on quickly—sticks could jab, rocks could crush. Now there was an even more powerful reason to keep the hands free.

The use of tools demanded a two-footed stance to give full play to the hands. This in turn created a need for a bone structure and musculature to provide continuous and effortless support. Finally, the development of an efficient coordinating center was favored: a bigger and better brain would be advantageous for making the most of the new posture and its tool-working possibilities. Some scientists believe that this series of developments—from ground life, to hands, to brain—is what motivated the development of human beings.

You can see why the bipedal nature of the snowcreatures has jarred members of the scientific community. As our theories of primate evolution now stand *we* are supposedly the only group of primates that *habitually* walks on two feet. If snowcreatures are bipeds, current thinking would make them close relatives of ours. Possibly, as some scientists and laypersons have proposed, they are an ancestral form of humans that has persisted to this day—a prehistoric leftover that somehow managed to survive into the twentieth century. If this sounds outrageous remember the coelecanth.

It is also possible that the snowcreatures represent a third line of development between apes and humans—creatures neither ape nor human, but sharing certain characteristics with both of them. Our collections of anthropoid fossils is rather sparse. It is entirely possible that this third line is lying buried in the rocks waiting to be discovered, or sleeping under a rhododendron bush in the Arun Valley.

Among possible snowcreature ancestors there are four most probable candidates: Gigantopithecus, Paranthropus, Homo erectus (Java and Peking Man), and Homo neanderthalensis (Neanderthal Man). Each has been proposed as the forerunner of the Abominable Snowcreature—or the living creature itself.

The discovery of Gigantopithecus dramatizes how little evidence is required to get scientists to believe in the existence of an unknown animal. In the 1930s, Dr. Ralph von Koenigswald, a Dutch geologist and paleontologist, discovered several unusually large ape-like teeth in a Chinese pharmacy in Hong Kong. The Chinese call these dragons' teeth and use them for medicinal purposes. What caught von Koenigswald's attention was the fact that these teeth were twice as large as the corresponding teeth in a gorilla! Based on his studies of the teeth alone he announced the existence of an entirely new species of fossil ape: Gigantopithecus, or Giant Ape.

In the four decades that have passed more of these giant teeth, and several jaw bones, have been unearthed. Altogether the evidence is modest, but enough to meet the demands of the scientific community. Gigantopithecus is in the literature and accepted as having once roamed the earth. In contrast, the snowcreatures, who have left their tracks all around the globe, and been seen by many hundreds of people, have not been accepted. It is easy to understand, though—the teeth can be held in your hand and examined, which is not the case with an eyewitness account of the yeti.

From the arrangement of its teeth and the cut of its jaw, paleontologists have reconstructed the size, form, and habits of Gigantopithecus. Its name derives from the early belief that these creatures stood 9 feet (2.7 meters) tall and carried corresponding bulk—perhaps as much as 600 pounds (272 kilograms). This awesome silhouette may have to be cut down somewhat. It is more likely that the giant teeth were set in a not-quite-so-giant frame.

The teeth, closely packed in the enormous jaws, were heavily coated with enamel. This dentition is best suited to resist the wearing effects of the powerful grinding action that Gigantopithecus applied to its diet of high-energy seeds and roots. In contrast, the teeth of living apes are only thinly enameled. Also, while the apes' incisors (front teeth) are used to nip and shred their food before chewing, those of Gigantopithecus are worn flat. They just picked up their food and chomped away immediately. In certain respects the teeth of Gigantopithecus resemble those of humans, who also have small, vertical incisors, broad flat molars, and reduced canines, all closely packed together. In fact, Clifford J. Jolly of New York University believes that the adopting of the graminivorous feeding pattern is the single most important event that began the separation of humans from apes.

How did these creatures travel about the grassy savannas? Most scientists lean toward the theory that Gigantopithecus was a knuckle-walker, like the present-day chimpanzee. It is not thought to have been a biped. But this is based only on examination of the creature's teeth and jaw bones! As it stands it is a very conjectural idea. The evidence really isn't in yet. It is just possible that the giant ape did in fact walk on two feet.

In summary, Gigantopithecus was a creature that was neither ape nor human. It belonged to a branch that separated from the two main lines of anthropoid evolution to go its own way. Descended from a forest ape, it took to the open savannas and roamed at least from China to the Siwalik Hills. These hills make up a part of the foothills of the Himalayas, interestingly enough. This giant lived in the very area that we are investigating. Putting all this information together, and relating it to what we know about the present-day snowcreature, Dr. Bernard Heuvelmans has come up with the theory that the yeti is a direct descendent of this ancient giant. The yeti's footprint, unlike either ape or human, lends weight to this view.

There is also the possibility that the yeti is not descended from Gigantopithecus, but is the very creature itself. Perhaps a population of these thought-to-be extinct animals managed to hang on for the last million years, past the life expectancy dictated by the fossils. The high mountain pastures that the yak frequents could conceivably supply the necessary food items required by Gigantopithecus. The deep river gorges and valleys could offer them shelter. The chances for this being the case seem remote, but not totally impossible.

The second possible yeti forerunners are known from their fossil deposits uncovered on the African continent. They are called Paranthropus. Controversy has accompanied these ancient creatures' standing in terms of their role in the human line of development. Paleontologists are divided on the question of how human-like they were. Some see them as an early link in the chain of human evolution, others as an unsuccessful offshoot.

The fossil evidence indicates that Paranthropus was bipedal,

74

but that it was not very good at this form of locomotion. It is believed to have been rather clumsy, reverting to a bear-like four-footed gait when pressured. Its teeth and jaws appear to be those of a vegetarian, and scientists think its feeding pattern was similar to the present-day gorilla's.

Taken as a whole, Paranthropus cuts a more human-like figure then its Asiatic cousin, Gigantopithecus. Although no Paranthropus fossils have been found in the Himalayas, it is still possible, if not likely, that the creature once lived there. If it did inhabit the Asian continent, it might very well have evolved into the present-day yeti. These two, the ape-like Gigantopithecus, and the more human-like Paranthropus, are the most likely ancestors of the Abominable Snowcreature.

We should also mention Homo erectus (Java and Peking Man) and the Neanderthals. Their names have been mentioned in connection with the snowcreature mystery and we must give them their due.

Both Java Man and the more advanced Peking Man were true humans. Their scientific name reflects this similarity: Homo erectus is in the same genus as the present-day human, Homo sapiens. The chances of this ancient species being an ancestor of the yeti are remote. Peking Man was a hunter of large game, a maker of stone tools, knowledgeable about fire and its value for survival (providing warmth, light, and the means for food preparation), and had a fairly large brain. All these facts taken together indicate that he was "quite an advanced human being," as John Napier notes.

The Neanderthals were even more refined. If decked out in boots and jeans you might pass one of them by on the street without thinking twice. The classic Neanderthals (there was an early and later type) were short and stubby, built like present-day Eskimos to conserve body heat. This was necessary because they lived through the last glacial advance and had to evolve a method of withstanding the cold, or perish. In addition to more refined tool-making and hunting capabilities, Neanderthals appear to have evolved their thought processes to the point where they could think about what happened to them after they died (we know they buried their dead with a good supply of food and weapons).

The ultimate fate of the Neanderthals is the basis for yet another scientific puzzle and debate. The fossil record shows a sudden disappearance of Neanderthal remains. Some scientists believe this resulted from their being exterminated by the more advanced Cro-Magnon people. Others believe that the Neanderthals interbred with Cro-Magnon people and so became part of the human heritage.

Both Homo erectus and Homo neanderthalensis were too highly evolved to be seriously considered as yeti ancestors. The lonesome yeti moving from valley to valley is too rough a creature to have descended from these more refined types. But they may play a role in the snowcreature story as a whole. It has been proposed by Russian scientists that some populations of Neanderthals managed to survive intact. As John Napier states, "It is not impossible that pockets of Neanderthalers living in remote regions of Eastern Europe, Siberia, and Mongolia could have avoided the consequences of either physical extermination or racial absorption and still be surviving as relic populations in these regions today."

Perhaps these Neanderthal survivors are the basis for the alma-type of snowcreature. Remember that these almas were described as being very human-like. Although there is no evidence at present to back up this contention, it cannot be ruled out as a real possibility.

During the next decade there may well be discoveries of

presently unknown and unsuspected fossil anthropoids. Perhaps one of these will better fit the snowcreature's hereditary picture. However, with the information we now have, the best explanation for the evolution of the yeti is through Gigantopithecus or Paranthropus. Since the remains of Gigantopithecus have already been uncovered in the Himalayan foothills, and we know nothing certain about Paranthropus' world-wide distribution, it would seem that the "giant one" is the most likely candidate.

Past, Present, and Future

Human beings have been addicted to storytelling since they first
began to speak. Some stories are meant to entertain, some to
please, some to frighten, and some to explain the mysteries of
life and creation. Take as a whole these stories form each society's mythic heritage. These myths attempt to make sense of a
powerful and commanding universe. In the twentieth century our
views on the significance of myths and folk tales have gone
through several changes. They are no longer regarded as childish and naive counterparts of modern science. They are no
longer dismissed merely because they seem to make no sense
when taken literally. Instead, it has been realized that these
myths represent a sizable and quite well organized body of
knowledge.

In fact, many advances in science, especially in nuclear
physics, seem to have gone full circle in coming to a world view

that is very similar to the religious and mythological beliefs of the Eastern religions. The problem with myths and folk tales is that the wisdom they contain is usually expressed in a language and logic that differs from our own. As Ivan Sanderson points out, many peoples in northern lands once explained the migration of swallows by assuming that when winter approached, these birds swam to the bottoms of lakes and ponds and went to sleep. Today we do not believe this, of course. It is not a scientific explanation of anything. It may seem very silly to us, except that it does contain two basic pieces of information that mesh with present biological concepts: these birds do disappear in cold weather and they must go someplace from which they can return in spring. Here is knowledge couched in colorful style.

In terms of the snowcreature, almost every culture has its stories of giants, wild people, and hairy types. In China (the land of Gigantopithecus), there are legends of a great stone ape who grew so powerful on earth that the Buddha himself had to put it in its place. Norse mythologies refer to a giant called Ymir, who was instrumental in the creation of humans. In ancient Greece there were stories that told of a race of giants capturing and devouring the god Dionysius. In turn, these giants were struck down by Zeus and humankind was raised from the ashes. In the Abo Settlement, a Pueblo village in New Mexico, there is a series of cave drawings depicting the footprints of humans and other animals found in the area. Among them are prints shaped like human feet but three times larger. In the Bible we read:

> There were giants in the earth in those days; and also after that, when the sons of God came unto the daughters of men, and they bore children to them, the same became mighty men which were of old, men of renown.

79

Are these simply stories created for their own sakes? Or do they, like the swallows at the bottom of the pond, imaginatively describe an historical-scientific truth? The core truth they seem to offer is that a race of giant human-like creatures once roamed the earth and interacted with human beings.

Once roamed, or still roaming? What happened to these giants? Either snowcreatures exist today or they are simply figments of the imagination. If imaginary, then at least they might be the mythical carry-over from an earlier time when such creatures actually did exist. If real, the snowcreatures must either be an abnormal strain of a known animal (what animal that might be is beyond me), a prehistoric form that managed to survive long past its assumed demise, or an unrecognized new member of the animal community.

The present evidence is inconclusive. There are few hard facts. That is, the skeleton of a snowcreature has never been unearthed, and not a single bone, tooth, piece of hair, or mound of excrement has been found that is generally accepted as belonging to him or her. Not a single photograph or frame of film has been universally accepted. The tracks are currently being debated over. None of the pieces of evidence relating to the snowcreature, either by itself or in combination, has been powerful enough to make a dent in the views of the established scientific community as a whole.

The strength of the yeti's case rests solely on circumstantial evidence—the eye-witness accounts and the controversial tracks. (Both are somewhat bolstered by mythological references to similar creatures.) Over the years, many hundreds of people have reported contact with snowcreatures or their footprints. The record in the Himalayas is strong. Could every single reported encounter with this elusive creature be attributable to hoax, misperception, or hallucination? Some of them, certainly.

Some of the Sherpas' stories were probably based on sightings of bears. Some of the tracks were probably made by bears or humans and distorted by the sun and wind. Many of the accounts are probably overly embellished fantasies, some are outright lies. But *all* of them?

The snowcreature controversy is at a critical stage. I believe the weight of the evidence merits a more serious investigation by the scientific community. At the present time there is a small but growing number of professionals who have taken the problem seriously. This is not to say that they believe in the snowcreature, just that they are willing to consider the matter. Among these researchers there is no consensus—some believe, some disbelieve. But at least one thing has been made clear, especially by John Napier's work: it is at least *possible* for the Abominable Snowcreature to exist in the Himalayas.

As with many other problems in science, bold and often intuitive strokes of faith are needed to leap past the bounds of logic and improbability to come up with a viable solution. Do we have enough of a case to make such a leap in proposing that the snowcreatures are real?

Many have claimed to see them. We have seen how they could survive in the Himalayan environment. We have proposed several alternatives to explain how they meet their dietary needs and provide shelter for themselves. We have seen how and where they could live, and demonstrated where they could have come from. In short, we have created a theoretical picture to account for their existence. You must now decide whether or not to make the leap. Remember, if only one of all the many tracks and sightings is genuine, then science will have to be rewritten to explain the creature behind it.

There is a strong dividing line between those who have lived in the Himalayas and those who have not. The Sherpas and

Tibetans who have evolved in the shadows of the mountains, and the visitors who have seen the vastness of the valleys, the denseness of the forests and the mysteries they hold, seem more ready to accept the reality of the snowcreature. For those who have come into close contact with nature's power and majesty, one more mystery is easy to absorb—here where nature is still untamed and a human remains a small creature.

Bibliography

Cohen, Daniel, *The Greatest Monsters in the World*. New York: Archway
   Paperbacks, 1977.
Cronin, Edward W., Jr., "The Yeti." *Atlantic*, vol. 236. no. 5 (Nov.
   1975).
Heuvelmans, Bernard, *On the Track of Unknown Animals*. New York:
   Hill & Wang, 1965.
Izzard, Ralph, *Innocent on Everest*. New York: E. P. Dutton & Co., Inc.,
   1954.
Kazami, Takehide, *The Himalayas*. Tokyo, New York, and San Francisco:
   Kodansha International, Ltd., 1968.
Napier, John, *Bigfoot*. New York: E. P. Dutton & Co., Inc., 1973.
Peissel, Michel, "Mustang, Remote Realm in Nepal." *National Geo-
   graphic*, vol. 128, no. 4 (Oct. 1965).
Reynolds, Vernon, *The Apes*. New York: E. P. Dutton & Co., Inc., 1967.
Sanderson, Ivan, *Abominable Snowmen: Legend Come to Life*. Philadel-
   phia and New York: Chilton Book Co., 1961.
Shipton, Eric, *The Mount Everest Reconnaissance Expedition, 1951*. New

Bibliography

York: E. P. Dutton & Co., Inc., 1953. London: Hodder & Stoughton, Ltd., 1952.

Simons, E. L., and Ettel, P. C., "Gigantopithecus." *Scientific American,* vol. 222 (Jan. 1970).

Tchernine, Odette, *The Yeti.* London: Neville Spearman, 1970.

Weidenreich, Franz, *Apes, Giants, and Man.* Chicago: University of Chicago Press, 1946.

Index

85

About the Author

Stephen Rudley is a Californian who currently makes his home in New York. He has taught science, has worked in the construction industry, and now devotes full time to writing and photography. His first book for young people was *Construction Industry Careers*.